C000001010

My Book of Riddles

My Book of Riddles

BLACK & WHITE PUBLISHING

First published 2018
by Black & White Publishing Ltd
Nautical House, 104 Commercial Street,
Edinburgh, EH6 6NF

1 3 5 7 9 10 8 6 4 2   18 19 20 21

ISBN: 978 1 910230 50 3

A CIP catalogue record for this book is available from
the British Library.

Typeset by Creative Link, Haddington
Printed and bound by Opolgraf, Poland

CONTENTS

INTRODUCTION

Ye'd better trim yer fingernails, cos I've come up wi' a batch o' real heid-scratchin' puzzles tae boggle yer brains. There are a' sorts o' teasers tae get ye thinkin' – number puzzles, word puzzles, logic puzzles – a' wi' a bit o' a Scottish twist. If ye get completely bamboozled, dinna worry – ye can check yer answers at the back o' the book. Best o' luck!

WULLIE

MATHS

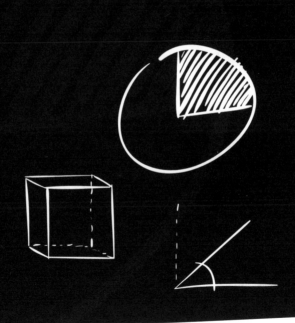

Whit's the easiest way tae mak
7 an even number?

If it taks ten men five hours tae
build a wa', how lang wid it tak
for five men tae build it?

If there are five neeps and
ye tak' awa' three, how many
dae you have?

When Maw went tae the bingo, out of 100 wifies 85 had handbags 60 had black shoes 75 had an umbrella 90 had their ain lucky pen. How many wifies must hae had all four items?

5

Ye want tae bile an egg for twa minutes but ye only hae three egg timers – one for three minutes, one for fower minutes and one for five minutes. How dae ye use these tae bile the egg for twa minutes?

6

Can ye help me wi' this
sum oor Teacher set us?
Using only subtraction and
multiplication get the answer
24 from 3, 6, 9 and 11.

7

Using only addition, how dae ye
add eight eights tae mak 1000?

How is the number
8,549,176,320 special?

A bat and a ball cost £1.10. The
bat costs £1 mair than the ball.
Whit does the ball cost?

Soapy Soutar was 9 twa days ago and he'll be 12 next year. Whit date is it?

Me and Fat Bob have pinched some apples. If Bob gies me one apple, we will both hae the same amount. If I gie Bob an apple, Bob will hae twice as many as me. How many apples do we each have?

How can ye add twa tae eleven
and get one?

In 2010 a lad was 5 years old.
In 2005 he was 10 years old.
How come?

Me and Soapy hae the same
number o' bools. How many do I
hae tae gie Soapy so that Soapy
has ten mair than me?

15

Soapy's pet snail starts climbin'
up a 30 ft wall. Every day it
climbs three feet but slips back
twa feet at night. How long will
it tak for the snail tae reach the
top o' the wall?

Using the letters of

TWO PLUS ELEVEN

Find another sum that gives
exactly the same answer.

Pa wants me tae chop a 20 ft tree trunk intae 20 logs one foot lang. It taks me one minute to chop one log. How lang will it tak tae hae the 20 logs?

I BET MA GI'ES ME THE MONEY FOR THAT COWBOY SET THE NICHT FOR ME BEIN' SAE GOOD TAE HER!

18

Mr and Mrs McTavish have five daughters. Each daughter has one brother. How many in the McTavish Family?

19

Oor butcher, Mr Lamb, is 5 ft 10 inches tall. Whit does he weigh?

Find the next twa numbers in the sequence

7 14 17 21 27 28 35 ? ?

WHIT AM I?

Whit dae I find easy tae get intae
but hard tae get oot o'?

Whit's bought by the yard and
worn by the foot?

I'm no' a plane, but I can fly through the sky. I'm no' a river, but I'm fu' o' water. Whit am I?

WHIT DAE YE CALL...

Whit dae ye call a lassie playing pool wi' three pints o' lager on her heid?

Name fower days that start wi' the letter T.

Wha scored a goal against
Scotland wi' a wooddin leg?

Whit dae ye call a man wi'
puffins and gulls nesting
in his pooches?

GEOGRAPHY

28

Explain how a tractor can be on
an island in the middle o' a deep
loch when it wasnae air-lifted
or taken by boat, there are no
bridges and the tractor wasnae
built on the island.

29

Whit three countries are hidin' in
the three sentences below?

As defendants we deny all charges.
I drop an amazing amount of
sweetie papers.
There's a bonnie loch in a valley.

IT MUST BE GREAT BEIN' A DUCK!-JUIST SWIMMIN' ABOOT LIKE THAT A' DAY AN' NAE SCHOOL!

30

Whit doesnae get ony wetter, no matter how much rain fa's on it?

I went tae Shetland on Valentine's Day and came back a week later on Valentine's Day. How did I manage that?

Afore Mount Everest wis discovered, whit was the highest mountain on earth?

Whit Scottish toons
are hidin' in the followin'
sentences?

Is thon hombre Chinese?

Can I hae the kipper that
Pa didnae eat?

Dinna wish away yer life.

Anither three toons hidin'
in these sentences.

The warm air dried Ma's
washin'.

Is that the call o' a
pheasant or a partridge?

I met Hilary McTavish in
the grocers.

35

A bus driver went through
a Stop sign wi'out stopping,
turned left past a No Left Turn
sign then went the wrang way
up a One Way Street, yet didnae
break the law. How?

In which month do fowk
sleep the least?

37

I beg your pardon.

I should learn not to overstay my welcome.

Tell the ornithologist I'm deeply sorry for the trouble caused.

It really is lamentable.

There are seven Scottish rivers hidden in these sentences. Can ye spot them?

WHIT AM I?

38

Whit's big and yellow and comes in the morning tae brighten Maw's day?

The mair ye tak, the mair ye leave behind. Whit am I?

Whit's black when ye get it, red when ye use it and white when ye're feenished wi' it?

Whit's aye coming but never arrives?

WHIT DAE YE CALL...

42

Whit does a tortoise call a lassie on his back?

Whit dae ye call a lassie wi' one
leg shorter than the other?

WORDPLAY

WoRD pLAy

44

Whit word o' five letters that ye use tae mak bread, is a form o' energy if ye remove the first letter, is something ye need tae do to live if ye tak awa' the first twa letters and is a drink if ye scramble the last three letters?

HERE COME THE DOTS

is a braw anagram for something
that means much the same.

46

Whit's the next letter
in this sequence?

M T W T F S ?

47

Whit starts wi' the
letter T, is filled wi' T
and ends in T?

Whit five letter word becomes
shorter when ye add twa letters
tae it?

RICHARD OSMAN'S YAK GUZZLED
BANANAS IN VENEZUELA

Whit does this strange phrase
mak me remember?

50 Pa uses the following clue tae mind his computer password. You Force Heaven To Be Empty. Whit's his password?

58

See if ye can work oot the
anagrams o' the words and
phrases below that mean
pretty much the opposite
o' the clues.

SANTA.
MORE TINY.
REAL FUN.
ILL FED.
FINE TONIC.

52

Whit word begins and ends wi' an E but only has one letter?

53

Whit's the next letter in this series?

O T T F F S S

Guess the next three letters in this series

G T N T L

55

Thon phrases below are pretty
much anagrams o' the answers.

A STEW, SIR?
MADE SURE.
SEA TERM.
IS NOT SOLACED.
TENDER NAMES.

Can ye think o' an eight letter word wi' only one vowel in it? Here's a clue – Desperate Dan has it.

57

Gie me a word wi' five consecutive
vowels in it. Here's a clue – Ma
hates doing it in the supermarket.

58

Poor fowk have it. Rich fowk need
it. If ye eat it ye die. Whit's the
answer?

59

Rearrange the following letters
tae spell just one word.

WUOETJSNROD

60

Can ye find the the mistake?

1 2 3 4 5 6 7 8 9

WHIT AM I?

The mair ye tak from me, the bigger I get. Whit am I?

At nicht I'm told whit to dae. In the morning I do as I was told. I'm no' all that popular. Whit am I?

Fill me up wi' water. I'll really heat things up. I'm no'a type o' beauty cream. But I'm braw at gettin' rid o' wrinkles. Whit am I?

WHIT DAE YE CALL...

Whit dae ye call a lassie standin' between twa goalposts?

65

Whit dae ye call a lad wi' a
poodle on his heid?

66

Whit dae ye call a lad withoot a
poodle on his heid?

CLASSIC RIDDLES

WE'RE GETTIN' WIR HALLOWEEN PAIRTY AT EDWIN'S HOOSE THE NICHT, I DINNA KEN WHAUR IT IS, BUT HE'S MEETIN' WIS HERE AT SEVEN THE NICHT! SO GET YER FACES BLACKENED AN' BRING TREACLE SCONES AN' A' THING!

67

A cowboy rides into town on Friday, stays for twa days then leaves on Friday. How come?

Twa people are born at exactly the
same moment yet they dinna hae
the same birthday. How come?

You walk into a room and find a pig
eating swill, a dog eating a bone
and a rabbit munchin' a carrot.
Wha's the cleverest in the room?

70

A muckle truck is crossing a bridge wan mile long. The bridge can only hold twa tons - the exact weight o' the truck. The truck maks it half way across the bridge and stops. A spuggie lands on the truck. Does the bridge fa' doon?

71

Four men were in a rowing boat on a loch. The boat turns ower, and all four men sink to the bottom o' the loch, yet not a single man got wet! How come?

72

A man pushes his car tae a hotel
and tells the owner he is bankrupt.
Why?

73

A man's in a room wi' twa doors.
If he goes through the first door
he will be instantly frazzled by
the sun shining through a pane
of magnified glass. If he goes
through the second door, he will
encounter a vicious fire-breathing
dragon. Whit should he dae?

74

Wee Eck bides on the tenth floor
o' a block o' flats. Every morning
he taks the lift doon tae the
groond floor and goes tae school.
When he comes hame he taks the
lift tae the sixth floor and taks
the stairs the rest o' the way.
Why?

75

Wee Eck's Maw has three bairns.
The first was called April, the
second May – whit was the third
bairn called?

76

Wullie, Fat Bob, Primrose Paterson and a muckle steak pie are at one side of a river. Primrose is a vegetarian and Wullie has promised her he won't leave her alone with Bob who keeps pulling her pigtails. Wullie has a rowing boat with enough room to take himself and one other person or thing. How can he get a'thing across the river without any pigtail pulling or pie eating?

77

A wifie dressed all in black is walking doon a country lane. A big black car comes roond the corner and screeches tae a halt. How did the driver see the wifie?

78

If a Red Hoose is made o' red bricks, a Blue Hoose wi' blue bricks, a Yellow Hoose wi' yellow bricks, whit is a Green Hoose made o'?

79

Twa mothers and twa daughters went into a café. They each ate one pie but only three pies were eaten. How come?

80

Twa Americans met for lunch. Ane was the father o' the other one's son. Whit relation were they tae each ither?

81

How can ye hud the twa ends o'
a piece a string and tie a knot
withoot lettin' go o' either end?

82

Ye're driving a bus. At the first stop, two wifies get on. The second stop, three men get on and one wifie gets off. At the third stop, three bairns and their maw get on, and a man gets off. The bus is grey, and it is raining outside. Whit colour are the bus driver's underpants?

WHIT AM I?

83

I hae fower identical brothers. While they get oot and aboot, I stay quietly in the dark and dae nothing. But in times of trouble I come oot and save the day. Whit am I?

84

I am a protector. I sit on a bridge. One person can see richt through me. While others wonder whit I hide. Whit am I?

85

I lose my heid in the morning, but get it back again at nicht. Whit am I?

MURDER/
MYSTERY

A cowboy hung up his hat and pit a hankie ower his een. He then walked 100 yards, turned roond, and shot a bullet through his hat. The hankie wisnae see-through – it completely blocked the cowboy's vision. How did he dae that?

87

Twa convicts are locked in a cell.
There is an unbarred windae high
up in the cell. No matter if they
stand on the bed or one on top
o' the other they cannae reach
the windae to escape. They then
decide to tunnel oot. However,
they gie up with the tunneling
because it will take ower lang.
Finally one of the convicts figures
out how to escape from the cell.
How d'they get oot?

Wee Eck
comes hame
tae find twa
deid bodies
on his flair
surrounded
by water and
shattered
glass. Whit's
been goin, on?

89

A mannie is trapped in a brick
room wi' no windaes or doors. All
he has is a saw and a plank o' wid.
How does he escape?

90

On which day o' the year dae
fewest people die?

91

A wifie is in a hotel room when she hears a knock on the door. When she answers it there's a complete stranger there who says: Sorry, missus, I thocht this was my room. He walks back doon the corridor and intae the lift. The wumman immediately phones the polis. Why?

92

Which room does a zombie avoid?

Is it legal for a man
in Aberdeen tae
marry his widow's
sister?

94

One Sunday afternoon Mr Toffington-Smythe was found deid in the drawing room. His missus said she was reading a book, his maid said she was cleaning the lavie, the chef said he was makin' breakfast and the butler said he was takin' a shower. Wha did it?

95

One winter's night, P. C. Murdoch
was in his hoose when a snowba'
crashed through his windae. He
raced outside to see Wullie, Soapy
Soutar and Mark Tamson running
roond the corner. He couldnae
tell wha had thrown the snowba'.
Primrose Paterson had witnessed
whit happened and put a note
through Murdoch's door. The note
said '?'. Wha threw the sowba'?

A wifie shoots her husband. Then she holds him under water for over 5 minutes. Finally, she hangs him. But 5 minutes later they both go out together and enjoy a braw dinner together. How come?

97

A lad was rushed intae the operating theatre wi appendicitis. The surgeon said: I cannot operate on this boy, he is my son. Yet, the surgeon was not the boy's father. How come?

98

Imagine you are about to be eaten
by The Loch Ness Monster. How
d'ye prevent it happening?

WHIT AM I?

99

I'm no' alive but I can grow. I canna breathe but I need air. I dinna hae a mooth and water kills me. Whit am I?

100

Tak off my skin and I winnae
cry – but you will. Whit am I?

ANSWERS

MATHS

1: Rub oot the 5.
2: Nae time at a' - it's already built by the ten men.
3: Three — the anes ye've just taken.
4: 10 (The difference between these numbers and 100 added together then taken away from 100 i.e. 15+ 40 + 25+ 10 = 90. (100 − 90 =10)
5: Turn the three and the five minute egg timers over while yer water biles. Once the three minute egg timer is empty, pit the egg in the biling water. When the five minute timer is empty, your egg has been biled for twa minutes. Oh, toss the four minute timer in the bin — ye dinna need it for this riddle!

6: $(6 - 3) \times 11 - 9 = 24$

7: $888+88+8+8+8= 1000$

8: It contains a'the single numbers in alphabetical order (if ye mak 0 = zero).

9: 5p

10: It's January 1st. Soapy's 10th birthday was on December 31st. Twa days ago he was 9 and next year on January 1st he will have turned 11 meaning he will be 12 that year.

11: Bob has 7 apples and Wullie has 5.

12: When you add twa hours to a clock, it becomes one.

13: He was living over two thousand years ago in BC.

14: Five bools. As long as Wullie has at least five bools to begin with.

15: 28 days – on the final day it wouldnae slip back.

16: TWELVE PLUS ONE

17: 19 minutes. The last chop will gie me twa logs.

18: There are eight McTavishs – Mr And Mrs, five daughters and one son. Each daughter has the same brother.

19: Meat.

20: 42 47 The numbers are either divisible by 7 or contain the number 7.

21: Trouble.

22: A carpet.

23: A cloud.

24: Beertrix Potter.

25: Tuesday, Thursday, Today and Tomorrow!

26: Steve Wooddin (New Zealand) in 1982.

27: Cliff.

GEOGRAPHY

28: It drove across thick ice in winter time.
29: As defendants we deny all charges.
   I drop an amazing amount of sweetie papers.
   There's a bonnie loch in a valley.
30: A loch.
31: Valentine's Day was the name o' the boat I sailed on.
32: Mount Everest – it just hadnae been discovered.
33: Is thon hombre Chinese?
   Can I hae the kipper that Pa didnae eat?
   Dinna wish away yer life.
34: The warm air dried Ma's washin'.
   Is that the call o' a pheasant or a partridge?
   I met Hilary McTavish in the grocers.
35: He wasnae in his bus, he was walkin'.
36: February, for obvious reasons.
37: I beg your pardon. I should learn not to overstay my welcome. Tell the ornithologist I'm deeply sorry for the trouble caused. It really is lamentable.
38: The school bus.
39: Footsteps.
40: Charcoal on yer barbeque.
41: Tomorrow.
42: Michelle.
43: Eileen.

WORDPLAY

44: WHEAT (heat, eat, tea)
45: THE MORSE CODE
46: S – the sequence is the First letter of the days o' the week.
47: A teapot.
48: SHORT
49: The colours o' the rainbow. The first letters o' this phrase help me mind Red Orange Yellow Green Blue Indigo Violet.
50: u472bmt (Say the phrase out loud)
51: SATAN
ENORMITY
FUNERAL
FILLED
INFECTION
52: Envelope.
53: E – The first letters of the first seven numbers, so the next number is Eight.
54: I T S – the initial letters of the question Guess the next three letters In This Series
55: WAITRESS
MEASURED
STEAMER
DISCONSOLATE
ENDEARMENTS
56: STRENGTH
57: QUEUEING
58: Nothing.
59: Just one word.

from rowing tae stop him!

77: It was the middle o' the day.

78: Glass.

79: They were a grandmother, mother and daughter.

80: Man and wife.

81: Before ye grab the string, cross yer arms. When ye uncross them ye'll tie a knot.

82: Whit ever colour yours are – cos you're the driver!

83: A spare tyre.

84: Sunglasses.

85: A pillow.

MURDER/MYSTERY

86: The cowboy hung his hat on the end o' the barrel o' his rifle.

87: They pile up a' the earth they dug frae the tunnel and climb up the pile o' earth and get oot the unbarred windae.

88: A goldfish bowl has been knocked over and the twa deid bodies are his pet fish.

89: He uses the saw tae cut the wid intae twa halves. Twa halves mak a whole. He crawls through the hole and escapes!

90: February 29th.

91: Because you wouldn't knock on the door if you thought the room was yours.

92: The LIVING room.

121

93: Certainly not. If his wife's a widow, he must be deid!
94: The chef. Why wid he be makin' breakfast in the afternoon?
95: Mark Tamson. Primrose's note meant Question Mark.
96: The wifie is a photographer. She shoots a photo develops it then hangs it up tae dry.
97: The surgeon was the lad's mither.
98: Stop imagining!
99: Fire.
100: An onion.

60: Look at the question – the word THE is used twice.
61: A hole.
62: An alarm clock
63: A steam iron.
64: Annette.
65: Doug.
66: Douglas.

CLASSIC RIDDLES

67: His horse's name is Friday.
68: One's born in Scotland, the ither in Australia.
69: You (hopefully)!
70: Naw. The truck has gone half a mile and used up a wee bitty petrol – keepin' the weight doon.
71: They were a' married!
72: He's playing Monopoly.
73: Wait till nicht time and go through the first door.
74: Because he's ower wee tae reach the lift buttons any heigher than six.
75: Wee Eck, of course.
76: Wullie rows Bob across the river and returns to pick up the pie. He drops off the pie and taks Bob back. He then leaves Bob and taks Primrose across leaving her with the pie before returning for Fat Bob.

FOOTNOTE: Bob eats the pie and pulls Primrose's pigtails and Wullie's ower puggled